Three step of success

QUESTION ,ANSWER ,WORK

Hello friends

Life is so good .donot waste it anywhere we have enough power that provide a inner power

Some important simple rule are given below '

1. TRY TO KNOW WHO ARE YOU-it is very simple question but answer is so hard .so you all deep think and then try to give answer .answer must be powerfull because you want success for this your thought is most important .may you have answer so you write first on a copy or notebook .i am ....ok

I think you all write answer the answer is I am a great powerfull soul or body that have enough power to build beatifull world . as you think or want fill it here......

2.try to keep great thought in mind-once you all think you are great body then it is your responsbility to think good and great .a single great thouht will provide you a lot of energy and change the future of your and your family .your great thought is ....

May be you think very well   .ithink your thought should be the solution of problem of old people and poor people .like how to change our politics.how to provide food for all. How remove viral and many more

3.time management-   good time management is the key of success . now you all have a great thought but only thought is not important for success .work on thought make them good .if we lost our time in thinking then you get some negative point on every thought and you will never start your work. Now make a time table that you can easily follow.

4- visualise big dream – look dream by open eyes .deep think which you want fill ……..
Then in aday think it and visulise it many more time it .and suppose this is you have .you got easily . The dream is that that make person sleepless. Said late APJ ABDUL KALAM former president of india

Now your work is so simple only read it and write so many times below it

5- donot fear to begin any work – every work that we are doing started by someone.

....
....
....
....
....
....
....
....

.....ok . I am power full. Repeat it five time.

6- donot expect help of anyone – I can do .iam powerfull .god help us. That is enough

....

....

....

....

....

....

....

....

....

....

.......yes, I am not helpless.

7- be happy – always try to live happy .happy mind have a constructive power that spreads around us. write down some reason.

I am happy because I am powerfull

I am happy because iam healthy

....
....
....
....
....
....many   more reason think and write .you are different from millions handicaps ,blinds ,patients that criminal that are unable to move on this beatifull earth.

8- BE THE CREATER OF YOURSELF

Now doing work with me you get some power so become the creater of yourself .your life live it according to your way .never give up from dream like animal . they have no thought that why their owner direct them take work as they wanted .but you are not animal .you are so powerfull human body and you have great thought .you already write down above.so write down below which you want become..

....

....

....

....

....

....

.... ok . I am ready to achieve my dream ..

9-solve the problem according to situtation

...problem---------------------solu-
tion...
....
....
....

....

10- accept the challenge of leadership- be the leader because the great architecture famous for their work not thousands worker named who work very hard with them.if you want change the nation then for that your ddecision is important .a good leader only take the right decision .

Ques- are you ready for this?

....
....
....
....
....ANS-yes yes yes

11- DO YOUR WORK ACCORDING TO YOUR ABIL-ITY- its you know what can you do? Other can only suggest to you what should you do ? mostly youth are misguide by their parents and teacher they said you can not do anything?

You take it and accept it .is it right?

No .....

It is not right. Recognize your talent and do work accordingn   that.one   thing   remember...
.... You are master piece in this world.

....
....
....now wirte your talent here   .
....
....
think daily one minute five times.

12-keep away from negative person and ideas---------
means if you keep away from negative persion then
you get 50% success . because these person take all
positive energy and make you energy less ., so first
write down the list of negative person.

....1......

2.......

3.......

4........

5..

Now say I am positive . I can .

13-keep your health good .----

Your success is directly depend on your hard work .hard work is depend on health and also good mental health is required for long time success .take vegetable and fruits more and join morning walk and zym .

....

....

....................now work

.... I will wake in the morning at .... Am

I will walk daily ..... km .

I will take rest after walking ....hours.

I will sung some song .

I will take fresh breakfast.

....

....................now say I am healthy.

14- work with rigidity=======…….

……………………………………………………………………………
……it   …………………….is
my………………………………………………………
…na-
ture……………………………………………………
…………………….my   personality
……………………………………is……………………………
…..mine.   i……………………………………….am
unique………..

15- concentrate on your aim -----

===
===== dreamless ....people are like ....animal...................your aim may change the life of millions............ so ....never ....destroy
....the future of millions........................now write your aim ....

Say I will fight for aim untill death...............................

16 – concentration is the key of suc-cess.--------...like light have seven colour and give brightness to other .it isway   to   achieve goal..
.............................if you spreads all power in-side you like some reading ,fight, discussion , then you will never achieve goal.every work take energy like   thiking   fighting   playing   .
....
....
....
....spending time is lost-ing already cocentration.....

17------mental power ---------------------- your mental power good .never think about you are weak in   mind.. your memory power is greater than million computer.../,.....................because   computer   is made by human .so human is strong than computer... ....keep in mind you areso powerfull .

Say I am powerfull. And my memory power is so good.

18----believe   on   yourself..
.......//////////////??????????????????????????????????????
??
??
??//////////////
yes yes yes yes yes yes

19------ life is a festival...enjoy every moment...sarrow and happy is part of life..

20----- take together to all
....your com-
pany is so good . you need to less work and ten-
tion...... strong bond of relation take away problem
....
....
....
....
....now say I am socially
adjustable...
....
....
....i am perfect.............

21----- be active ....if we are active in life then never comes negative thought . disturbing person always keep away . one day we become the most successful person of the world...ok ....now repeat

I am powerfull human body.,,,...............postive ....great thought...........concentrate on a great goal ....live together. ....beleive on myself . I am success.

....

22- LIVE IN GOOD ENVIROMENT—for good health and you have to live in good enviroment where more oxygen for breathing . good breathing makes good brain . you should attach with nature . walk with nature and talk with nature .

....

.... I am taking oath......................... To make a piece-full enviroment .... I will plant so many tree in year.....................................

23---help to other----.

World so wide some people have talent but lack of guideness they misguide .if help to them they also become and make change the nastion...................so today I am taking a oath to ....my self ....i ....will help a people in my whole day .... Help is way by which we connect to myself to other

....
....
....
....
....
....ok   yes yes

24----no problem are permanent-----

Dear friend in life no problem is permanent .it is good to know I have a super power . that give the solution   of   all   problem   ./////// ....no   prob- blem.. ....it is so good . god is great . I have done most   of   the   creative   thing   ., ...so I am a great problem solver.

Yes .i can...........................

25—enjoy your success ------

Enjoy your ability but never become eagerness on anyone .donot shadow on anyone happyness .

....
..............................so my thought enjoy your success . it will reduce the your temptation . I will change one of the most matter.............................. your.

....
....
.... byou should enjoy yourself.

Shailendra pratap yadav

www.ingramcontent.com/pod-product-compliance
Lightning Source LLC
Chambersburg PA
CBHW022127150726
47991CB00008B/3113